# THE NORFOLK BRO

## A Portrait in Old Picture Postcards

by

Basil Gowen

Foreword by Tony Scase

S. B. Publications
1990

# CONTENTS

# CONTENTS CONTINUED



S.B. Publications.

# ACKNOWLEDGEMENTS

Many people in Broadland, including relatives and friends, have been helpful to me in the writing of this book and I shall be forever indebted to them all. No-one has been unwilling to give me information, in fact the only time dissention has occurred was when two separate gentlemen took exception to 'authority' referring to drainage windmills as 'windpumps' and marshes as 'wetlands' and I must admit, in spite of my references in this book, that I am on their side. I would however like to especially thank:

Bett, my dear wife – for her constant support, her constructive criticism and for putting me right on at least two occasions.

Mr. John W. Neville and for the loan of 4 postcards from his collection, see pages 12, 14, 15 and 16.
Mr. Charles Lewis, Curator and the staff of Great Yarmouth Maritime Museum.
Mr. & Mrs. Sargeant, Stokesby Community Office & Store.
The Broads Authority, in particular Miss Jess Tunstall.
Mr. Frank Cooper and Mr. Graham Cooper
Mr. Stephen Earl of The Norfolk Windmill Trust.
Mr. Barry Johnson and Mr. Roy Detheridge.
The staff of Lowestoft Library.
The staff of Norwich City Library (Local Studies section)
The staff of Norwich Weather Centre.
Mr. & Mrs. Perry, Acle Post Office.
Messrs. Kelly's Directories Ltd.
Steve Benz for editing and marketing
Mr. Owen A. Needham
Mr. John Walker
Mr. Douglas Iredale
Mr. Fred Brown.
Mr. Gordon Curtis.
Mr. R. Haylett.
Mr. R. C. Mutten.
Mr. Billy Nudd.
Mr. Monty Pitkin.
Mr. Laurie Sayer.
Mr. G. Southgate.
Mr. Philip Standley.
Mrs. Dorothy Debbage.
Ms. Shirley Court.
Mr. Michael Sparkes.

If this small book has aroused your interest in collecting old postcards of your own neighbourhood, assistance can be found by contacting local postcard dealers or by joining the Norfolk Postcard Club who meet every second Wednesday in the month (except August) at The Assembly Rooms, Theatre Street, Norwich at 7 p.m. Meetings commence at 7.30 p.m.

# FOREWORD
## by
## Tony Scase
### Journalist and broadcaster

My fondest memory of the Broads was when I padded through the undergrowth of Wheatfen Broad in the footsteps of the late Ted Ellis in the early hours of the morning. Ted moved with the confidence of a man who knew every inch of the reeds, dykes and broadland waterways. I was convinced I would be swallowed up in the darkness or at least come to an inglorious end in a watery grave.

As the sun came up, glinting on the rippling water, the Broads came to life. Birds swooped and dived. Pochard, great-crested grebe, coot and even a heron put in an appearance as our television cameras turned. Ted, a naturalist without equal, provided a dawn commentary, a mixture of eloquence and enthusiasm. His words enhanced the beauty of the Broads, which I discovered to my surprise, were not the creation of nature but the work of mediæval peat diggers.

Thousands of people sail, cruise and fish on the Broads under a wide-horizoned sky. To some it is just a pleasurable day out. To others the exploration of a wonderful landscape, with unexpected sights and sounds unfolding in a journey of discovery. Today the major industry caters for yachtsmen and holidaymakers. Reeds are still harvested and stacked for thatchers. But the trading days of the wherries, the black-sailed barges which carried farm produce and household supplies, are over. Windpumps, however, still survive, a reminder of the drainage efforts of the hardy reclaimers of the marshes before electric pumps came into being.

Basil Gowen's love of the Broads is reflected in his choice of evocative pictures. Many postcard collectors have cause to be thankful for his eye for detail, his authoritative guidance and his lively interest in social history. The golden age of postcards from the turn of the century onwards captured the rich, vivid pattern of life on the Broads. Basil's journey along the unique waterways, aided by an army of postcard photographers, will delight those who know the Broads well and appeal to those making their first visit to this special corner of East Anglia.

*Tony Scase*
*Congham,*
*King's Lynn*

# INTRODUCTION

The Norfolk Broads, which I will immediately accept as also being partly in Suffolk, provide that geographical feature which East Anglia shares with Holland, large areas, just below sea level of boggy, marshy ground, susceptible to sea flooding. For centuries, mankind has waged a constant battle with the North Sea, fighting to keep what he has reclaimed. Historians tell us that Romans coming to this area sailed their galleys into a large estuary, around some islands coming up nearly as far as Acle. The invading Danish Norsemen, the Vikings, made their camps, or 'bei' on the higher firmer ground and so today we have Stokesby, Scratby, Oby, Ormesby, Hemsby, Filby and Rollesby here in the East Flegg District of Norfolk. Peat diggings, which created 'turf ponds' were the result of the efforts of bygone Broadland inhabitants to keep themselves warm and to supplement their wood fires, but subsequently as alternative fuels became available, this practice ceased.

The Broads, as we know them today are the deeper parts and still filled with fresh water, but as 'infill' has progressed over the centuries, the reduction in Broadland water continues. In the shallow waters, sedge can readily establish themselves which in turn encourages the growth of alder and sallow and ultimately the introduction of birch and oak. Contemporary writers tell us that no one knows the original extent of the Broads, but in the last one hundred and fifty years, their water has been reduced by half. Of course not all of the land is inhabitable, often providing not more than grazing for cattle. In World War II the Government paid farmers to plough up hundreds of acres of marshland to grow crops and help the war effort. In the post-war period most of this land seems to have been returned to grazing. Over the last century, the Broads have developed as an area for recreation, yachting, shooting, fishing and even ice skating during those very occasional winters when the Broads were frozen over.

In more recent times, from the turn of the century, the area has witnessed the growth of the holiday industry providing an area where the 'townie' can enjoy the peace and tranquility of the flat expanses of open water, marshes or reed beds. The additional pursuits or hobbies of fishing, birdwatching even sunbathing, have all added to the pleasure of a 'Holiday on the Broads'. It has become obvious to locals and visitors alike, that with the ever increasing use of the facility of the Broads, which was created as a National Park in 1989, that some other effective control and management than that provided by the existing Broads Authority is required in an area which is submerged by the huge influx of holidaymakers each summer.

My purpose in writing this book, however, is not to criticise visitors to this area, after all 'swede bashers' contribute to similar problems wherever they take their holidays, but to illustrate by means of old postcards how some places in Broadland used to look. I was born in a village beside the River Bure which can be said to link the two main areas of the Broads. I have many happy memories of my childhood from fishing to 'dyke jumping' when the latter practice occasioned many a ducking or at best, wet feet. I hope these pictures from the past taken from my collection of old Norfolk postcards, which I have accumulated over ten to fifteen years, will give you as much pleasure as I have had when selecting them for this book.

I have sought guidance as to our route round the Broads from widely differing sources, from the books of the late William A. Dutt, whose Norfolk of 1903–4 contrasted sharply with my own home county, and to the R.A.C.. However, I have decided to adopt the suggestion of my son Paul, who spends much of his business and private life poring over maps. Our route therefore, starts from Wroxham; the acknowledged 'Queen of the Broads' and certainly the centre of Broadland with its boat builders and boat-hire firms. Then west to Hoveton, Belaugh, Coltishall (not navigable beyond), and Hautbois before returning south-west through Wroxham again to Salhouse Broad, Horning, Ranworth, South Walsham and St. Benet's Abbey. From there the route makes a detour north with a brief journey along the River Ant, How Hill (Ludham), Barton Broad, Stalham and Sutton, and retracing the River Thurne to Ludham and Womack Water, Potter Heigham, Martham, Hickling and Horsey. The journey is resumed along the River Bure to Thurne, Thurne Mouth and Acle, with a detour via Muckfleet (not navigable) to Filby, Rollesby and Ormesby Broads, then retracing along the River Bure to Stokesby, Stracey Arms and Great Yarmouth (Yacht Station only). Leaving Great Yarmouth via Breydon Water, past Berney Arms windmill, Reedham, the River Chet and Loddon, Cantley, Buckenham, Brundall, Surlingham, Bramerton, Postwick and Thorpe to Norwich (Riverside). A return is then made along the River Yare by Haddiscoe Cut to St. Olaves, Somerleyton and Herringfleet, diverting along the River Waveney to Beccles, back to Oulton Broad and ending the journey at Lowestoft.

Have a pleasant trip. Imagine that you are on holiday and don't forget your camera, remember that not everyone had one fifty to a hundred years ago; hence the reason for so many old postcards. If any reader has any reminiscence or comment to make in relation to any information given in this book and inserted after careful research, I would be delighted to hear from them.

*Basil Gowen*
*Norwich*
*April 1990*

# MAP OF THE NORFOLK BROADS

Not to scale

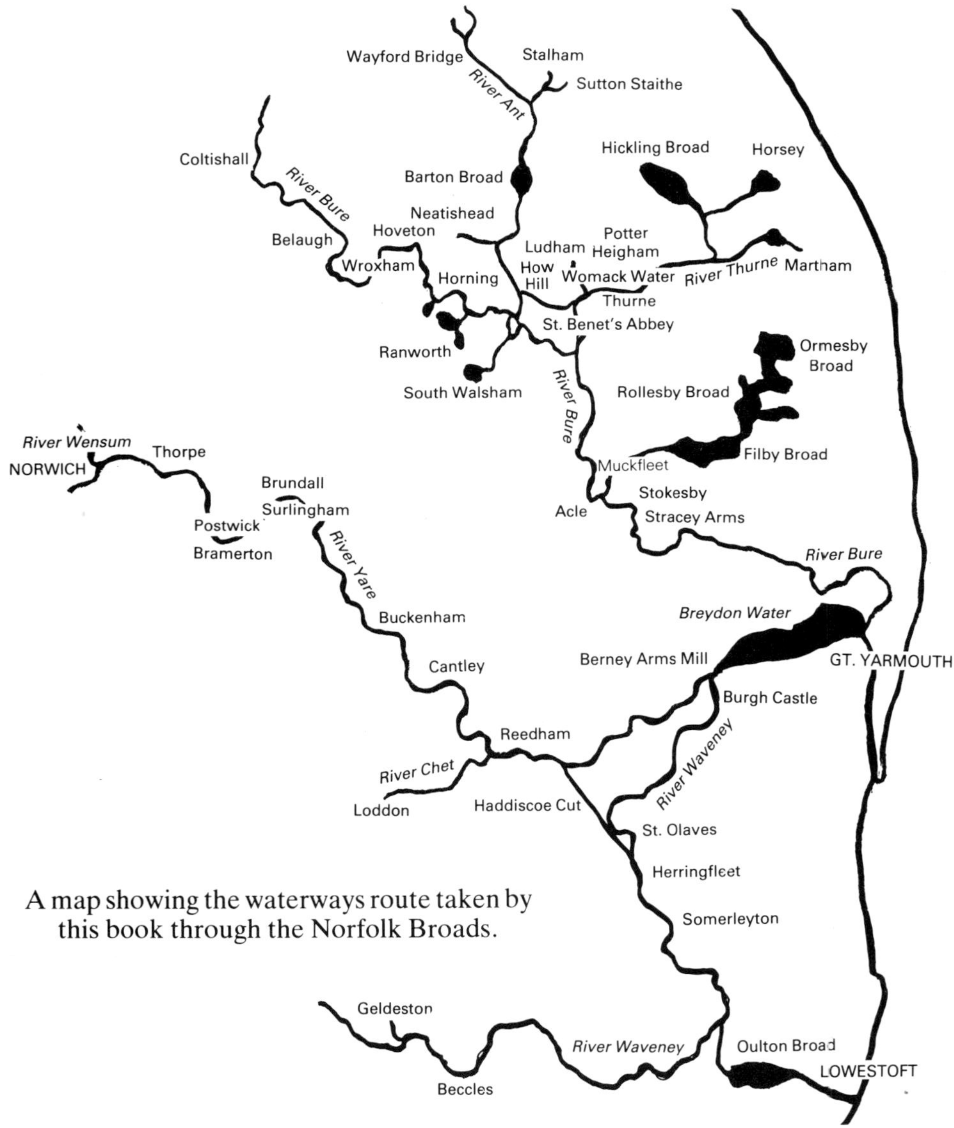


A map showing the waterways route taken by this book through the Norfolk Broads.

**WROXHAM BRIDGE, c. 1938**

Wroxham – the Queen of the Broads – has grown considerably this century as a direct result from the growth of the leisure industry. This has lead to the building of hotels, and many river-craft hire firms and boat-builders setting up in business to keep pace with demand. Census returns record the population as 374 in 1881, 624 in 1944, and 1,438 (with 186 in Hoveton) in 1988. This postcard was used by a G.I. to write home to his family in Ohio, U.S.A.. In addition to carrying a military censor mark, the message on the reverse reads: "Today, I have come down to this place for a swim and have had quite a time".

**WROXHAM BRIDGE, c. 1904**

The first bridge was built of wood in 1596, replaced by a brick structure in 1614, and rebuilt in 1897. In 1968, due to the increase in volume of motor traffic and the weight of modern vehicles, the bridge was reconstructed by laying a steel structure over the top with a separate walkway for pedestrians. The bridge carries a warning notice for all approaching river traffic: "To sound horn and lower windscreen before proceeding under". This view shows John Loynes' boatyard, left background, which designed and built boats and sailing craft specially for the Broads. He also advertised wherries, yachts, launches and boats of all descriptions for hire. On the right, today, out of view, is the Hotel Wroxham, shopping complex and post office. Jeckell's, sail-makers, established in 1832, and Ernest Collins' boatyard are also situated in Wroxham.

**THE BOAT-HIRE INDUSTRY, WROXHAM, c. 1948**

A publicity postcard published by Thornycroft advertising one of their splendid 40ft-long cruisers and various other craft built for the boat-hire industry on the Broads. The rapid growth of the industry led to central booking agencies being established. By 1937, Blakes Ltd. of London were representing thirty Norfolk Broads boat owners. Hire charges for boating holidays vary according to the time of the season, with the high season dated between 24th July and 28th August. In 1937, the cost per week to hire a 6-berth cruiser in the high season was £16–£18. Today, the equivalent cost would be in excess of £300. Daily hire charges (1990) are £7 per hour (inclusive of V.A.T. and fuel) or £33 for eight hours.

**S.S. "QUEEN OF THE BROADS", Nr. WROXHAM, c. 1912**

The *Queen of the Broads* and her sister-ship, the *Pride of the Yare* (see page 107), were built at Critton's Yard, Great Yarmouth in 1889 and 1892 respectively. Their specifications were 74ft length, 13ft beam and 5ft draught and both pleasure-steamers were owned by the Yarmouth and Gorleston Steamboat Company Ltd. Every weekday from June to September, the *Queen of the Broads* departed from Town Hall Quay, Great Yarmouth and travelled to Wroxham with up to 180 passengers on board: the 65-mile return journey costing only a few shillings. During the journey, when approaching river bends or Broadland villages, she would sound her horn to warn river traffic of her proximity and resultant passing swell, and also to alert villagers she was in the vicinity. During school holidays, local children would assemble on the quayside and invite her passengers to throw pennies at them; the old penny was quite heavy and could hurt if you were not agile enough to duck or someone's aim was better than you thought! After many years service, this much-loved steamer was withdrawn and broken up in 1976.

**ROYS OF WROXHAM, c. 1930s**

Messrs. Arnold and Alfred Roy opened their first store in Coltishall in 1895 (see page 11). Their business flourished and later they opened other stores in Horning, Potter Heigham and Wroxham. Roys of Wroxham advertised themselves as "The World's Largest Village Store". The multi-view postcard shows many of the buildings occupied by Roys in the centre of the village. Top left: Point House formerly the drapery and millinery dept., now the d.i.y. dept.. Bottom left: clothing and shoe dept., now the garden centre. Top right: the Norfolk Broads Shopping Centre housing the wines and spirits dept. and offices. The building in the background housed the ironmongery, furniture, china and glass and electrical depts.. These have both been demolished to accommodate a road improvement scheme, and a department store and bank now occupy the site. Bottom right: Roys Pharmacy now occupied in part by Miss Roy, ladies fashions. Centre: Arnold House formerly the grocery dept.. The magnificent art deco fascia has now been removed and the building houses a large supermarket. Today, the stores at Coltishall, Horning and Potter Heigham have closed and Roys of Wroxham (actually situated in Hoveton) is run by Mr. Fred Roy, son of the late Alfred Roy.

**HOVETON, Nr. WROXHAM, c.1920s**

Photographed from Wroxham Bridge and looking down Norwich Road towards the junctions of Church and Stalham Roads, in the far distance. On the left, the tallest building, was occupied by Roys Fish Stores. Point House, the three-gabled building shown centre right, was occupied by Roys drapery dept.. The tailoring, boots and shoes dept. occupied a single-storey building to the rear. In the right foreground, the white kiosk was known as 'The Newspaper Supply Service and Visitors Enquiry Bureau'. Chamberlin postcards – referring to the advertisement on the side of the kiosk – were produced by John George Chamberlin who was sub-postmaster until the 1920s. Notice the lad tinkering with his bike and, further down, the ice-cream cart. Today, many shops in Wroxham only cater for summer visitors and close during the winter months.

**NORWICH ROAD, HOVETON, c. 1927**

A later view of Norwich Road and showing the alterations that had taken place on the right-hand side of the road; the trees have been cut down and new buildings constructed in their place. In the right foreground, Sidney James Stringer established his business as a cycle dealer in the early 1920s. Later he sold motor-cycles and by 1925, his business occupation was registered as a motor engineer. Today, Stringer's building has changed only slightly in appearance, but is now occupied as a café and fancy goods shop.

**HOVETON, c. 1925**

Ward's Telegraphic Stores and Wroxham Post Office stood on the corner of Norwich and Station Roads. At the time of this photograph, Miss Ward was the sub-postmistress and Mrs. Emma Rosa Ward owned the grocery stores next door. The corner of Roys Pharmacy can just be seen on the right of the picture. Today there have been substantial alterations and these buildings are now occupied by Miss Roy, ladies fashions. The village newsagents, Stringer's, and part of Wroxham Bridge can be seen in the left background. The splendid convertible tourer and the two motor-cycle combinations probably relied on Stringer's to keep going!

**NORWICH ROAD, HOVETON, c. 1935**

In addition to the noticeable increase in motor traffic, a number of interesting changes have occurred including the erection of the art deco fascia to Roys Store, the addition of a new telephone box, many flagpoles and numerous advertising boards reflecting the increasing number of holidaymakers visiting Wroxham. The Eastern Counties 'bus, reg. no. VG 3352, on its way from Yarmouth to London via Norwich and Newmarket, passes through while visitors shop for postcards or gaze idly at the activity on the river. Notice the signs for the various newspapers on sale at the newsagents, in the right foreground, many of which are no longer published, e.g. Sunday Pictorial, Chronicle, Sunday News, Graphic, Dispatch and Empire News.

**ON THE BURE, WROXHAM, c. 1912**

An idyllic scene of early Broadland cruising. A pleasure wherry and dinghy – probably hired from Loynes' boatyard – leaves the quayside close to Wroxham Bridge. The hirer steers while the crew hoist the gaff sail. Usually, the larger boats had two permanent crew members for the duration of the hire: the 'skipper', responsible for navigation and seamanship, and the 'steward' who did all the cooking and cleaning. Notice the fisherman, in the left foreground, with the young swans gathered round him waiting for bread or spare bait. Let us hope that he was careful with his spare lead-shot weights; the use of which is now illegal. The view on the right has changed completely. Today, the site is occupied by the Hotel Wroxham, a shopping precinct and an adjoining car park.

**THE STREET, COLTISHALL, c. 1908**

The population of Coltishall was 952 in 1881, 916 in 1901 and 1622 in 1988 (inclusive of parishes absorbed). At the turn of the century, the village amenities included a hotel, five public houses, a cottage hospital and a railway station on the branch of the East Norfolk Western Extension Railway (Wroxham – Aylsham); at the time the stationmaster was Richard J. Read. The Roy brothers (see page 5) commenced their 'empire' here in 1895. Notice their hardware store on the left and their grocery and drapery store on the right. The fascia board shows that they had already opened one of their other stores in Wroxham. Closer examination of the picture reveals a baker's delivery cart under the trees, a lovely old gas lamp outside Roys' hardware stores and a workman up a ladder repairing some guttering. Today, apart from modernisation and different ownership of shops, the street is unchanged. Four trees still stand despite recent gales.

**COLTISHALL, c. 1910**

The Rising Sun public house was owned by Bullards brewery of Norwich. At the time of this picture, Henry Goodson was the licensee. On the left are the Staithe Granaries belonging to Ling & Co., corn, coal, cake, seed and salt merchants. On the right, just out of view, stands the King's Head public house. Today, there has been extensive modernization and redevelopment. The Rising Sun is part of the Chef and Brewer group owned by Grand Metropolitan Retailing Ltd. The King's Head still stands, and the two inns now have a large joint car park to the right of the picture, also out of view.

**THE ANCHOR HOTEL, COLTISHALL, c. 1932**

The Anchor Hotel was always a favourite stopping-place for a drink or a good meal. During the 1930s, the landlord was George Raymond Neal. The 'Anchor' is now closed and was converted to a private residence in c. 1985.

**COLTISHALL, c. 1913**

The Wesleyan Chapel Band, relatives and friends about to depart on their annual Sunday School outing. The entire party were transported to Mundesley by four horse-drawn waggons loaned by local farmers and millers: the waggon, shown above, was loaned by Hines and Wright. In the evening, on their return journey, the entire party were drenched with pouring rain; a disappointing end to what must have been one of the highlights of their year. The Chapel band disbanded at the outbreak of the First World War, when many of its members enlisted to fight for their country. In the background, the flint and brick building is the Methodist Chapel which still exists today.

**ROBERT HOOK, COLTISHALL, c. 1905**

Robert Hook was a general and horticultural builder, carpenter, wheelwright and hot-water engineer – a real jack-of-all-trades. This early photograph, overprinted for use as a Christmas greetings postcard, shows his yard in Rectory Road. Notice the tree trunk ready for sawing into planks, and various items for sale including a rather grand garden shed complete with two finials on its gable ends. Note also two employees standing rigidly to attention with their fixed gaze!

**THE LOCK, COLTISHALL, c. 1910**

Coltishall was described by Mr. William A. Dutt in 1903 as being 'the most picturesque waterside village in the district'. He described the Lock as 'nearly as picturesque as the one at Flatford on the Stour'. This is the limit of navigation on the Bure and even in Dutt's day it was never navigable to its source at Melton Constable. There were three more locks then, between Coltishall and Aylsham upstream. Notice the lock-keeper's cottage, on the right, which does not exist today.

**GREAT HAUTBOIS AND LITTLE HAUTBOIS, c. 1934**

In 1901, Great Hautbois had a population of 145 and came under the administration of Coltishall. Little Hautbois nearby was described as 'a decayed village'. Today, statistically, they are part of Coltishall and Buxton respectively. The postcard shows the grounds of Great Hautbois House owned by Mrs. F.E. Patteson. She was patron to both the local Girl Guides and Scouts: the tents shown in the photograph probably occupied by one of the organisations. Today, Great Hautbois House is the East Anglian H.Q. of the Girl Guides Association. The River Bure is too shallow here for navigation by larger boats, but the area is ideal for fishing.

**FARMAN BROTHERS, SALHOUSE, c. 1912**

The thatching yard of Farman Brothers, basket-makers, reed merchants and thatchers, situated close to Salhouse Broad which covers 40 acres. Norfolk reed *(Phragmites communis)*, which is not only confined to Norfolk, provides the best thatching material in the world, lasting at least 70 years. Fathoms of reeds – bundles six feet in circumference – were transported by wherry or reed-lighters (flat-bottomed punts) to a thatching yard. Reed beds were cut annually because if they were left to grow, they became "double wild" and unsuitable for good thatching. The postcard shows the neatly-stacked rows of sways, liggers and broaches: the fixings for thatched roofs. Sways are hazel or willow poles used to hold the layers of thatch in place. Liggers are similar but thinner and used on the roof apex and ridge. Broaches made of hazel or chestnut are thatching spars and hold the sways in place. They would be cut into bundles, 2ft 2ins long, soaked in barrels and cut and bent into a staple shape. Thatching would take place between April and October, the sways and broaches prepared before Christmas, and the reeds cut after Christmas until the spring. The craft of thatching is still very much in demand with family skills handed down to each generation.

**THE FERRY BOAT INN, HORNING, c. 1914**

For many years the Ferry Boat Inn has been a popular meeting place for yachtsmen, visitors and locals alike. During the Second World War it also became a place to relax for R.A.F. personnel from the nearby airfield at Coltishall. On the evening of Saturday, 26th April, 1941 at 9.45 p.m., the 'Ferry Inn' sustained a direct hit from a German raider which had been shadowed by a British fighter plane. The raider dropped fifteen bombs, one of which destroyed the inn. Casualties were heavy. Fourteen civilians and six R.A.F. personnel were killed including the pub barman, Mr. Henry Sutton of the well-known Gt. Yarmouth fish-curing firm, two of his sons, a daughter-in-law and a niece. There were eight injuries including the landlord, Mr. A.R. Stringer. Next morning, the British pilot, on surveying the aftermath, conjectured whether the German pilot had become aware that he was being tailed and had decided to lighten his bomb load. Local rumour has it that car lights (even with the restricted wartime lighting) had reflected on the inn's white walls and pin-pointed the building as an aerial target. Today, the Ferry Inn is as popular as ever.

**HORNING, c. 1925**

The Swan Hotel, shown on the left, was built in 1897. It offers excellent accommodation and food and provides its guests with first-class aspects of river activities. Today, the 'Swan' is part of the Chef and Brewer group. In the centre, the malthouses, owned by R.S. Watling & Son, were demolished in 1928. On the extreme right, the Yacht Station belongs to Southgates and still thrives today.

**THE STREET, HORNING, c. 1920**

The population in Horning was 435 in 1881, 557 in 1921 and 1,145 in 1988. In the centre foreground, the bakery and the grocery shop belonged to Benjamin Sims. Notice the fine display of enamel advertising signs: Caley's milk chocolate, Cadbury's chocolate and Home and Colonial tea. Today, the Street has many reed-thatched cottages, private houses and shops; the latter benefiting from the influx of visitors during the summer months. The businesses include a butcher, dress shops, art and craft shops and a grocer.

**A FISHERMAN'S TALE, HORNING, c. 1950**

An 'angler', not even dressed for the part, displays his giant catch, plus the one that got away! The two boys seem unimpressed and concentrate on landing a tiddler! Photographed looking towards the quay heading of the Ferry Inn (see page 19). Notice the house-boat, with its sun deck on top, moored against the far bank.

**HORNING**

A watercolour postcard depicting the Broads of yesteryear: goods and pleasure wherries, yachts and Horning Ferry smock mill. This was used as a drainage mill, also known as a windpump, to control the level of water on low-lying land or marshes. Notice the marsh-man using the tail-pole to turn the sails into the wind. The mill is now a private residence. A Norfolk drainage mill can be recognised by its typical boat-shaped cap. The basic machinery of shafts and driving-wheels lead to a scoop wheel, located either inside or outside the mill. The scoop wheel, turning in a trough, would push the water through a sluice gate into the tail race which discharged into the river: the sluice gate opening automatically by the pressure of water behind it. At normal working speed a scoop wheel could lift approximately 7 to 8 tons of water per minute, adequate for most requirements except bad floods. Another drainage mill existed at Horning Ferry. It was different in design and known as an open trestle mill (see page 31). The mill closed and became derelict.

**R.C. LOCKETT, HORNING, c. 1905**

R.C. Lockett was a merchant selling reeds, rushes, fodder, hay, straw, coal, chaff and general forage. The photograph of his yard shows a grindstone and stock-piled fathoms of reeds ready for transportation, some of which are being loaded on to a horse-drawn cart. Today, in Horning Street, a house named 'Locketts' stands on the site where the business was located.

**MILLS STAITHE, RANWORTH, c. 1904**

A transom-stern wherry tied up at the quay heading for loading. The hatches have been removed and probably stacked near the cuddy (crew's quarters at the rear). To facilitate loading, the long gaff has been swung to one side and made fast to a tree on the opposite quay heading. A large maltings was established here by Messrs. Mealing and Mills in the late 19th century. The nearby public house, built in 1762, was called 'The Jolly Malsters' in 1881, but is now known as The Malsters Inn and managed by the Chef and Brewer group. Close by is The Broadlands Conservation Centre, run by The Norfolk Naturalists Trust, which includes a seven-mile nature trail. St. Helen's church in the village has one of the finest rood screens in England, dating from the mid-fifteenth century. There is a superb view from the top of the church tower.

**SOUTH WALSHAM BROAD, c. 1900**

A typical scene at the turn of this century. A bowler-hatted old gentleman, clay-pipe in his mouth, surveys his domain. A holidaymaker rests on his oars and a fishing keep net, with other fishing accoutrements, completes the picture. This Raphael Tuck and Sons card from their 1900 'Norfolk' series was chosen by the Norfolk Postcard Club as being the most representative of the area, and is used as their club emblem.

**FLEET DYKE, SOUTH WALSHAM, c. 1923**

Another Broadland industry is sedge or rush gathering. The rushes are used for thatching (see page 33) or bedding for cattle. A Mr. William Parker was in business as a litter merchant in the village at this time. The population of South Walsham has remained under 600 for the last hundred years.

**PRATT'S OLD CURIOSITY SHOP, SOUTH WALSHAM, c. 1912**

Mr. Frederick J. Pratt commenced his business as an antiques and antique furniture dealer in 1890. The Old Curiosity Shop was built in 1905 and situated in Broad Lane. The business still trades today as Leo Pratt & Son. The Curiosity Shop, managed by Mr. Rodney F. Pratt, grandson of the founder. The shop is well worth a visit and can be found by leaving the B1140 and taking the road to South Walsham Broad. On arrival, visitors will find a veritable 'Aladdin's Cave'.

THURNE MOUTH 104

**THURNE MOUTH**

The wide expanse of water at Thurne Mouth makes it an ideal place for racing and regattas. The Thurne Mouth Open Regatta Committee organised regattas between the wars and during the 1950s and 1960s. Other local sailing clubs also organised races and festivities in their areas, including fairground amusements; generally known as Regatta Week. After the Second World War, the clubs concentrated more on yacht racing and the additional festivities associated with Regatta Week declined. Today, Regatta Weeks are held at Wroxham and Horning. The other sailing clubs at Acle, Hickling and Thurne Mouth hold their race meetings over a weekend or two or three days.

**THURNE DYKE**

This is an ideal place for mooring overnight, just off the mainstream. Thurne Dyke Mill, shown on the right, is a well-known landmark for those who travel on the Broads. The windpump was backwinded in 1919 and the whole of the cap, sails and most of its machinery fell into the marsh. It was repaired in 1920 but by the end of the war it had fallen into disrepair. The windpump was restored by Mr. R.D. Morse and is now leased to the Norfolk Windmills Trust based in Norwich. The windpump, one of two at Thurne, is situated on the east bank of the river at the entrance to Thurne Dyke, and open as a museum during summer months. Over seventy windpumps, either restored or derelict, still remain in the Broads area today.

**HOW HILL STAITHE, Nr. LUDHAM**

A fully-laden trading wherry on the shallow waters of the River Ant. Notice the necessary precaution of removing her 'slipping keel' which is being towed in the water alongside her. In the background is How Hill Mill, also known as Boardman's Mill, a late 19th-century trestle-windpump and converted from scoop-wheel to turbine pump in 1926. It is one of the Norfolk Windmill Trust's showpieces, open daily and well worth a visit. How Hill Nature Reserve nearby has bird hides, wildlife of all descriptions, a water trail and Toad Hole Cottage – an eel catcher's home built a century ago, and recently restored by the Broads Authority. The privately-owned gardens are open to the public on selected Sundays during May only. Visitors are rewarded with a spectacular show especially when the rhododendrons are in full bloom.

**BARTON BROAD**

A watercolour postcard depicting Barton Broad painted by Stephen John Batchelder. Born in Bolton, Lancashire on 17th January, 1849, he went to school in Preston, and in his early teens, the family moved to Great Yarmouth where his father set up a photographic business. When financial difficulties beset the firm, young Batchelder took employment as a photographer's assistant, whilst still attending Yarmouth School of Art when work would allow. Married at the age of nineteen, he had five children, and lived at 7, Garrison Road, Great Yarmouth. Eventually, he took over his employer's business, but in 1882 when the shop lease expired, he decided to devote all his time to painting and sketching, which he did for the next forty-seven years until failing eyesight forced his retirement. He specialised in Broadland scenes but also painted Great Yarmouth, Norwich and other areas of the county. His best work is said to have been between 1880 and 1900 and he had many exhibitions in Norwich. Today, his paintings and postcard reproduction of his work are collected by all who love Broadland and Norfolk.

**BARTON BROAD, c. 1900**

Barton Broad covers up to 100 acres. This early scene shows two moored wherries, a variety of smaller craft, and litter or sedge gathering by horse and cart. Sedge *(Carex spp.)* is used for constructing a ridge when thatching a roof. Norfolk reed, although the best roofing material, is unsuitable for this purpose. Sedge is more pliable and can be bent over the apex of a roof.

**STALHAM DYKE, c. 1930**

Showing one of the tributaries of the River Ant. The boathouse, shown on the left, would afford 'some' protection from the elements and be in use throughout the year. In the background, the date of construction of the corn mill at the Staithe is unknown, but the first reference is on Bryant's map of Norfolk 1826 and the builder accredited to be Dan England. Census returns for Stalham record the population as 852 in 1881, 937 in 1921 and 2,894 in 1988.

**HIGH STREET, STALHAM, c. 1908**

Mrs. Emily Cattermoul with members of her family standing outside the village post office. She also ran a grocery, drapery and stationery business from here. By c. 1910, she had given up her position of sub-postmistress to concentrate on managing the shop full time. Miss H.E. Furrance became the new sub-postmistress. The photographer must have amused the group in some way to capture such delightful expressions, especially the children.

**THE STAITHE, SUTTON, 1908**

Many acres of glebe in this area, abounding in reed and sedge and known as 'the poor man's fen', were let annually to provide money for 'the poor coal'. The river and stream were kept free of vegetation to ensure drainage. In 1908, when this view was taken, boats of shallow draught were used to transport the reed. In the foreground, notice the young lad on his tricycle and in the background, the stack of reeds against the building.

**THE RIVER ANT, Nr. LUDHAM BRIDGE, c. 1909**

Looking down the River Ant towards Ludham Bridge, shown in the left background. This peaceful and tranquil location, with the river giving access to the nearby village, is very popular with holidaymakers. On the right, a pleasure wherry is moored by the bank, and behind, a windpump which was demolished in the 1950s. Two other windpumps can be seen on the skyline. Over the years, many windpumps were replaced by steam pumps, later replaced by electric pumps: one drainage pump powered by electricity could do the work of several windpumps. Ultimately, many mills were abandoned as they were uneconomic to keep in operation.

**LUDHAM BRIDGE, c. 1938**

An active scene at Parkinson's Yacht Station, Ludham Bridge. The stores, on the right, sold provisions, newspapers, cigarettes, and Esso petrol. They also offered river trips and possibly boats for hire. Today, the scene has changed completely. The only structure left is the windpump, formerly Ludham Bridge North Side tower mill, now derelict and without its cap. The shop has been replaced by 'The Ludham Bridge Store', standing fifty yards away from the river and facing the road, supplying chandlery, fishing bait and general provisions.

**THE DOG INN, LUDHAM, c. 1925**

Standing about a quarter of a mile from the Bridge and situated on the A1062, The Dog Inn is very handy for locals and visitors alike in the summer months. The landlord at the time of the photograph was Richard Basil Geary. The population of Ludham was 796 in 1881, 759 in 1921 and 1,304 in 1988. Today, 'The Dog' has changed structurally. The low single-storey building to the left has been demolished, the front of the building now has a single-storey flat roofed extension, and at the rear on the right, a single-storey building has been built and used as a family room. The area in front of the family room is now the car park.

**LUDHAM, c. 1911**

Roughly one mile from the Bridge at Stocks Hill stood the premises of George Samuel Knights, saddler and harness-maker, ironmonger, and shoemaker's grindery. Standing in the doorway with his two assistants on the right, he displays a glorious array of his wares: tin baths, buckets, ropes, rakes, horse-collars and saddles. Today, the building still stands on the A1062 and is now 'The Craftsman' restaurant.

**WOMACK BROAD, LUDHAM, c. 1912**

Once a small Broad, this is now a collection of channels known as Womack Water. The famous black-sailed wherry *Albion* is moored here. For many years it was the only surviving trading wherry on the Broads. These wherries carried timber, grain, marl, reeds, rushes, sand and coal. However, their main cargoes were sugar beet, transported to Cantley Factory (see pages 94–95), and, up to the 1920s, malt. The *Albion* is available for hire by groups of people today.

**WAYFORD BRIDGE, c. 1930**

Wayford Bridge is situated one-and-a-half miles to the east of Stalham. At the turn of the century, the navigable River Ant afforded facilities for landing coal, malt, corn and other kinds of merchandise. Several firms set up depots to handle trade. Today, this area has been transformed by the construction of the A149 Stalham bypass to Caister-on-Sea, including a new bridge which was completed in c. 1968. Boat-hire firms offering daily hire, light engineering works and refreshment facilities have also been established here. The Wood Farm Inn, a popular public house, stands close to Wayford Bridge.

**HUNSETT MILL, STALHAM, c. 1938**

Over the years, Hunsett Mill has become one of the most photographed windpumps in Broadland because of its setting and accessibility. The tower mill was built in 1860 and is now privately owned. Notice the boathouse in front of the mill and the marsh-man's cottage on the right. The sailing boat is rigged with a standing lug sail.

**POTTER HEIGHAM, c. 1950**

Many Broadland holidays start from Potter Heigham. The village has become an extremely popular area as it offers so many facilities for holidaymakers. The Bridge, centre left, is an awe-inspiring target for many a newcomer when hiring a motor-cruiser for the first time. Many decide to stay downstream of the bridge until they are more proficient, but if you should hire from a firm further upstream you had no choice but to pass under the bridge. (The author speaks from personal experience!) In return for a pint, any driver in trouble could always call on the assembled locals to free their boat jammed under the bridge. However, during daylight hours and when tides are favourable, pilots from Pennant's, Blakes or Hoseasons are available to pilot hired cruisers under the bridge.

**THE BRIDGE, POTTER HEIGHAM, c. 1919**

A close-up of the Bridge over the River Thurne with assembled onlookers, visitors and locals; a fine place on a summer evening to stand and watch the world go by. The bridge is believed to have been built in c. 1380, with the brick parapets dating from the 18th-century. For many years, the narrow width of road over the Bridge, resulted in a bottle-neck causing regular delays for traffic wishing to cross the Bridge. In spite of the recent bypass diverting vehicles clear of the village, crossings are still controlled by traffic lights. The Bridge Hotel can be seen in the right background.

**THE QUAY, POTTER HEIGHAM, c. 1950**

A view of Herbert Woods Ltd. quay heading in the right foreground. Across the river, the two white buildings belong to the boat-hire firm of Geoffrey Applegate Jnr. The population of the village was 414 in 1881, 516 in 1921 and 858 in 1988.

**THE BRIDGE STORES, POTTER HEIGHAM, c. 1937**

The Bridge Stores were well known to Broadland visitors and locals. The proprietor at this time was Sidney William Gerrard. The stores were also the collection point for express parcel deliveries via the Eastern Counties Bus Company. Outside the stores, in the left foreground, an intriguing leader on the newspaper board reads: "False nose clue in murder mystery". Another sign by the penny-in-the-slot weighing-machine advertises the availability of hot rolls every morning. The stores were situated on the main Stalham to Great Yarmouth road which leads over the Bridge (pages 44–45) and shown above in the right background. Today, the A149 bypass has relieved many of the traffic problems in the village.

**GRAPES WATER-MILL, POTTER HEIGHAM, c. 1903**

The water-mill was owned by Charles Grapes whose occupation was listed as a marsh mill-man. The picture certainly gives an impression of the bleakness, especially in mid-winter, of a marsh-man's life on the Broads at the turn of this century. The message on the reverse of this card from Kitty to her friend at Frinton-on-Sea reads: "Do you recognise this mill of Flo's?".

**POTTER HEIGHAM, c. 1912**

A view of the junction of Ludham and Stalham Roads, with Station Road in the left background. The proprietor of the corner shop was James Watts who sold groceries, provisions, drapery, haberdashery, boots, shoes and patent medicines. Later, he built a tea room and a dark-room on the left-hand side of the shop. It looks as if the photographer has deliberately waited for a train to arrive to ensure plenty of animation for the picture. The postcard is from his own series and printed by Jarrolds of Norwich. Today, the building is known as the Post Office Stores and owned by J & A. Holland; the post office housed in a single-storey extension at the side of the building. The house in the background still stands.

**EEL-FISHER'S HUT, POTTER HEIGHAM, c. 1910**

Eel fishing occurred between July and August – the breeding season. As this was a seasonal activity, most eel fishers had other occupations. When the eels were 'moving', the fishermen would remain in this type of hut (often a converted boat) for days on end. They stored their catch in boxes, pierced with small breathing-holes, submerged in the river. The best catches occurred after a full moon and on a very windy night, when the moving reeds made the eels restless. A good-sized eel weighed 6–7lbs and a worthwhile catch weighed fifty stone; this only happened on rare occasions. When the catch was sufficient, it would be despatched to Billingsgate Market in London. Small catches were distributed locally. The cash received would be sufficient for only a few weeks. At the end of the season, many fishermen would return to factory work at Cantley (see pages 94 – 95) during the winter months.

**THE FERRY, MARTHAM, c. 1912**

The ferry over the River Thurne consisted of a movable pontoon which could be positioned either to allow people to cross the river, or moved aside to allow river craft to pass through the gap. The postcard shows the pontoon being manoeuvred into position by two boys. The punt in the foreground may have been used either as a ferry or along the shallow waters of the nearby drains – drainage ditches or dykes. The population of Martham was 1,093 in 1881, 1,335 in 1921 and 2,985 in 1988.

**MARTHAM, c. 1910**

Looking down White Street and showing Mrs. Olivia S. Pyman's shop which sold groceries, general provisions and hardware. The single-storey building next door was a butcher's shop owned by Herbert William Jeary. His delivery cart can be seen parked in front of his shop. Today, Pyman's shop has been demolished and the butcher's shop is occupied by J. Ward. Martham is a large village on high ground giving good views of the surrounding Broads. If one visits St. Mary's Church, there is a fascinating inscription on a slab in the church tower partially obscured by the organ. It was written in c. 1730 by Christopher Burraway who commemorated his wife Alice with the words: "In this life my sister, my mistress, my mother and my wife." Burraway was an illegitimate child of an incestuous union between his father and his sister. To hide the disgrace the child was placed in the Foundling Hospital. Many years later he returned to Martham and was employed as a farm labourer by his mother-sister. By sheer hard work he later became the farm bailiff and eventually married his employer (mistress). After their marriage, she discovered his identity by noticing a familiar birth mark on his shoulder! They both never recovered from the shock of this discovery and died shortly afterwards.

**MARTHAM, c. 1930**

The windpump in the background is Martham Level tower mill. It was built in 1908 and converted to residential use in the 1950s. The sudden appearance of a wherry or yacht's sail crossing an open flat landscape must have caused consternation to many motor-car drivers. The author remembers the reaction of a Geordie friend, during his first visit to Norfolk and when driving round a bend in the road, who had to be heard to be believed!

**HICKLING BROAD, c. 1910**

The largest of all the Broads, its huge expanse of open fresh water was said in 1989 to cover 1,200 acres (nearly two square miles) but other estimates are more conservative. Without doubt, it is a haven for yachting enthusiasts. The postcard shows preparations for the annual Regatta, which was held traditionally during the first week in August. The wherry, slightly left of centre, flying pennant and flags is the 'Committee Boat'. The Judges' boat is shown on the extreme right of the picture. Hickling Broad is the location of a nature reserve run by Norfolk Naturalists' Trust; a bird-watcher's paradise, with many walking trails offering peace and tranquility.

**MOORINGS AT THE STAITHE, HICKLING, c. 1950s**

This is 'Back Dyke' behind the Pleasure Boat Inn. Most of the area is now occupied by the public house, its car park, and the Whispering Reeds Boat Co. Ltd. whose boats are hired out by Hoseasons Holidays. The boat on the right is one of the fleet belonging to Herbert Woods of Potter Heigham. The 6-berth cruiser *Queen of Hearts,* in the centre, is one of the fleet belonging to Jenner's of Thorpe. Notice the boats' registration numbers. B723 and Y408; the letter denoting the home base of the owners, e.g. B – Bure, W – Wensum, Y – Yare. During the 1950s, when the number of boats became too numerous, a different system of registration was adopted.

**THE PLEASURE BOAT INN AND STAITHE, HICKLING, c. 1909**

In 1904 the landlord was George Beales Jnr., and in 1912 the landlord was Harry Carpenter. Notice the attractive garden between the dyke and the building. Early in World War 1 this was removed to allow contractors to have access to the far end of the rond to construct a concrete slipway. The military authorities had decided to use Hickling Broad as a reserve base for flying boats. Even when rough weather prevented take off at the airbase at Great Yarmouth, Hickling Broad was never used as an operational base. Today, the inn has been renamed The Pleasure Boat and is managed by the Chef and Brewer groups. The main building remains unchanged structurally but the single-storey building to the right has been rebuilt to extend the dining area.

A PRETTY CORNER, WEST SOMERTON

**WEST SOMERTON, c. 1920**

The two wherries were owned by the brothers, Dionysius and Sidney Thain who were farmers, coal and corn merchants. The Thain family were also connected with wherry transportation for many decades. From the neat appearance of the two wherries, both vessels were undergoing a refit or being repainted; their name boards, rigging and other fittings have been removed. West Somerton tower mill, in the left background, was built in 1900 by Dan England. The mill still stands today but is now derelict. Nearby in the village, in St. Mary's churchyard, is the tomb of Robert Hales, the Norfolk giant 7 feet 8 inches tall, who died in 1863.

**THE STAITHE AND HORSEY MILL, HORSEY, c. 1950**

This wide stream is a tributary of the River Thurne and is navigable. The North Sea lies roughly a mile away to the east. Horsey Mill dates back to the early eighteenth century and was originally known as Horsey Black Mill. It lost its cap in 1895 and the mill was rebuilt in 1912 by Dan England. In 1943, the mill was struck by lightning which split the sail stocks. These were not repaired until 1957 and Horsey Mill is now under the care of the National Trust. It is open daily during the summer from June to September, when visitors can climb the tower and view the old machinery. The surrounding marshland is a recognised breeding ground for marsh birds, insects and plants. This is also under the care of the National Trust.

**THE SEA FLOODS, HORSEY, 1938**

On the night of 12th February, 1938, a North Sea surge broke through the sand-dune defences between Winterton and Sea Palling. This view shows the actual point of the breach. Some fifteen square miles of low-lying marshland area were inundated. Many homes were affected, and thousands of freshwater fish were killed by the effects of the salt water entering the Broads. On the 3rd April, 1938, the temporary seal of the breach was again broken and further work had to be done to effect a more permanent repair.

**THE SEA FLOODS, HORSEY, 1938**

Work being carried out at the point of the breach, which was sealed finally by 14th May. However, the repair remained a problem for the Authorities for many years. The Anglian Water Authority is responsible for many hundreds of miles of coastline. During the night of 31st January, 1953, an exceptionally high tide, eight feet above normal, backed by a north-east gale, resulted in another surge which caused a serious breach in the sea defences at Sea Palling Gap, three miles north-west of Horsey, and at many other places along the East Coast. Over three hundred people drowned (including seven at Sea Palling and nine at Great Yarmouth), thousands of cattle, sheep, pigs and poultry perished, and thousands of acres were flooded. The surge also caused serious damage to the coastline of Belgium and Holland resulting in the loss of over two thousand lives.

**ASHBY-WITH-OBY, c. 1920**

This area is situated in the parish of Ashby-with-Oby. Ashby was described as a 'decayed village' in 1881. The area today is almost exclusively devoted to farming and the necessary labour requirements of local farmers reflect the rise and fall of the population: 107 in 1881, 178 in 1921, and 47 in 1988. Oby Mill was built in 1753; the first brick-built mill in Norfolk. The River Bure is quite wide here and is part of the course used for Acle Regatta.

**"AWAY FROM IT ALL", ACLE, June 1915**

Many family photographs were printed and used as postcards. This example shows a family from Shropshire on holiday, having moored their boat on the banks of the River Bure, at a spot where the rushes had been cut, just upstream from Acle Bridge. They are enjoying afternoon tea and the writer tells her girl friend: "We are getting bonny and brown". One wonders how they could do so wearing all those clothes! It is a sobering thought that at the time this peaceful scene was photographed, many thousands of young men were being killed or wounded across the North Sea in Belgium and Northern France.

**THE RIVER BURE FROM ACLE BRIDGE, c. 1914**

The dayboat rigged with its four-sided mainsail and jib belonged to Mr. John Walter Eastick; his boatyard and boat-hire business were situated just upstream and on the opposite side of Acle Bridge from where this view was taken. The postcard had been posted on 30th August, 1914 to Pte. Ernest Eastick who had just joined the 6th Battalion Norfolk Cyclist Regiment at North Walsham. His sister informed him that the boats had done nothing during the first month of the war. In the left background is St. Margaret's Mill, another drainage windpump. In c. 1960, it was converted into a private residence by the actor John Glyn Jones. In c. 1972, it was sold and became St. Margaret's Mill Restaurant. The proprietor is Mr. B. Kennard.

**THE BRIDGE INN, ACLE, c. 1914**

During the 1920s, the landlord of the Bridge Inn was Tom George who handed the licence on to his daughter and son-in-law, Dolly and Fred Leach. Between the Wars, the area between the inn and the main road was the site for the annual 'Rhubarb' Underwood Funfair which preceded or coincided with Acle Regatta. The funfair attended the various regattas in Broadland and was very popular with the younger generation. After the Second World War, the exterior and surrounding area of the Bridge Inn were smartened up. The inn now has a large car park to the right of the main entrance. On the postcard, notice the unusual design of the weighing-machine complete with handrails.

**ACLE BRIDGE, c. 1920s**

Acle Bridge, with its three spans, was built in c. 1880. Increasing motor traffic on the A1064, which crosses the bridge, caused constant bottle-necks during the summer season. This resulted in the bridge becoming inadequate and having to be replaced. The advertisement for cooked fowls refers to a speciality of The Bridge Inn nearby.

**ACLE BRIDGE, c. 1937**

The new bridge was built between c. 1928 and 1931. It has a single span and two lanes for traffic above. The postcard shows a driver of an Austin 12 who has stopped to admire the view – an impossibility today in high summer with the many parking restrictions.

**PROVISION STORE, ACLE BRIDGE, c. 1936**

The business was started by Mr. Ernest Noah Curtis in the 1920s. Mr. Curtis and his wife also owned the stores in Billockby, situated about a mile away along the A1064. In 1946, Mr. Curtis handed the business over to his son, Gordon, who lived in a house close by which bore this unusual sign on the gate: *Be ye man or be ye woman; Be ye going or be ye comin'; Be ye early or be ye late; Be ye sure to shut this gate.* The shop made sales and deliveries by launch to holidaymakers moored along the river-bank. This photograph was taken during one of his deliveries! The newspaper flysheets suggest interesting reading: News of the World – "The Glory that is Britain"; News Chronicle – "Yarmouth on the air tonight"; The Times – "King's Health improving"; Daily Mail – "King's Health" and "Britain's Spain Plan". The business was taken over by Gordon Curtis' daughter, Janet, and her husband Frank Howard in 1983.

**OLD ROAD, ACLE, c. 1910**

The smithy was owned by John Wilkerson, who is shown standing by the entrance with his assistant, Sidney King, and the 'boy'. He became a master farrier in c. 1900 and retired as village blacksmith in 1931. At this time, business was brisk and the blacksmith was a valued member of the village community. The smithy contained two forges and four horses could be worked on at the same time. Today, the smithy has been demolished and in its place stand Roy Wilkinson's shop selling general goods and fishing tackle, and, to the right, Carter's family butchers. Forge Cottage stands on the left-hand side of the stores.

**THE STREET, ACLE, 1910**

This picture was probably taken on market day held every Thursday. There is certainly plenty of activity. Sandell's Supply Stores sold grocery, provisions, millinery and drapery. Notice the superb window display of Camp coffee and the advertisements for Churchmans counter shag and Delicious tea – special blend – priced at 1/10d (11p) per pound! Next door is The King's Head Inn serving Youngs, Crawshay and Youngs ales and stouts – the licensee James William Wright. Further down is the Queen's Head commercial hotel whose licensee was Samuel W. Richmond. Today, Sandell's is occupied by Milltance, ironmongers, The King's Head still serves pints, and the Queen's Head, since 1977, is the office of the Woolwich Building Society and Acle Video Centre. A bus shelter and public toilets have been erected in the space between the two public houses.

**THE WATER-MILL, STOKESBY, c. 1930**

The Commission Mill, a drainage windpump, was built by William Rust and stands at the mouth of the Muckfleet where it joins the River Bure. Up to 1920, there was consideration that this stream could be opened up to permit the passage of smaller craft to Filby, Ormesby and Rollesby Broads. This idea was dropped finally when the Stokesby 'New Road' and a new bridge were constructed. By the 1930s, the Muckfleet was unnavigable, even for a rowing boat, because of a dam-grid across its mouth. Today, the stream is choked with weed.

**THE BRIDGE, FILBY ROAD, c. 1910**

In reality, the three Broads of Filby, Ormesby and Rollesby are one large expanse of water intersected by the A1064 Acle – Caister-on-Sea road and the A149 Stalham – Caister-on-Sea road. This view shows the bridge at Filby looking in the direction towards Caister-on-Sea and Great Yarmouth. Today the bridge is much the same, except for the addition of a pedestrian walkway on the left.

**THE LANDING-STAGE, SPORTSMAN'S ARMS, ORMESBY, c. 1910**

The landing-stage at The Sportsman's Arms public house; the landlord at the time was William Richmond. The Sportsman's Arms also had pleasure grounds beside the Broad and catered for boating, fishing and picnic parties. During the 1920s the public house was renamed the Eel's Foot.

**ROLLESBY POST OFFICE, c. 1914**

At the time of this picture, Samuel Arthur Gibbs was not only the sub-postmaster but also the village blacksmith. In 1925, Mr. Walter James Miller Snr. became sub-postmaster. Later, his son took over the position, and in 1986, his daughter, Mrs. Gallant became sub-postmistress. A new post office/stores was built behind the building shown above, facing the A149. Today, the old post office is occupied as a private house owned by Mr. & Mrs. Gallant; all the ivy has now been removed.

**COCKLE'S POINT, STOKESBY, c. 1930**

On the left, the now dilapidated sailless cornmill was owned by a smallholder, Ted Youngs, and the greenhouses by a market gardener, Friday Cumby. The low flint-stone building, second from the right, was occupied by the village blacksmith, Jack Earl, with one operating forge. This postcard is from the series published by Mrs. Emma Elizabeth Gowen who was sub-postmistress at the post office at the time. The post office was on the Green which is not in view. The population of the village was 331 in 1881, 311 in 1921, and 271 in 1988.

**STOKESBY, c. 1930**

The Provision Stores, owned by Elizabeth and Ralph Simpson and situated at Riverside, were very popular and convenient for visitors 'on the river'. The Simpson's car, a Morris 12 reg. no. EX 2964, stands in the foreground. Also, notice the tinned goods piled on shelves in the window and the row of vending machines alongside selling chocolate and cigarettes. Sadly, Ralph Simpson was one of the first men in the village to give his life for his country serving in R.A.S.C. in World War 2. Today, the building has been converted to a private house.

**STOKESBY, c. 1931**

The Provision Stores owned by Mr. Bertie Osborne were used by visitors and locals; one of three stores in the village at this time. The tall shop sign was placed so that it could be seen from a distance. When the Osborne family sold the premises to Mrs. Shaljian in c. 1937, it became the village post office and general stores. Today a 'Community Office' is used as a part-time post office, opened two days a week, and sited at the other end of the village (see page 78). The Candle Cavern and Craft Centre is located in this building today.

**THE FERRY INN, STOKESBY, c. 1914**

This public house was known as The Ferry House when Elijah Thurtle was the proprietor in 1883. In 1905 it was renamed The Ferry Boat Inn, and later at about the time this picture was taken, when Robert Edgar Allen was the proprietor, it was renamed The Ferry Inn. Today, it is known as The Stokesby Ferry. The ferry crossing-point can be seen on the left, but by this time it was virtually disused because of the new road to Acle. During the extreme winter of 1940, when the Bure and the Broads froze over, it was possible to walk across the river at this point, in fact, skating became popular for a few weeks in Broadland! Notice the splendid open-top tourer outside the inn. E. Lacon and Co. Ltd. of Great Yarmouth owned the pub at this time and today it is owned by Whitbread and Co. of London.

**STOKESBY, c. 1915**

This view shows the centre of the village. On the left, behind the white railings, is William Fowler's carpenter's shop and yard, and behind the hedge, left of centre, is the Green. Edward Trett's corn windmill can be seen behind the houses in the left background. The building in the centre was built as a Wesleyan Methodist Chapel in 1811, with an adjoining caretaker's house. In 1927, the Methodist purchased the Primitive Methodist Chapel at the other end of the village street and the old chapel became the home of Mr. W. 'Dojun' Green, with part of the building used as The Conservative Club. After the Second World War, the building was bought by the village and used as the Memorial Hall. It was demolished in 1986 and is now the site of a fresh fish shop. Between the house on the extreme right and the fish shop today stands the Stokesby Community Office and Bungalow Stores run by Mr. and Mrs. W.A. Sargeant. Since February 1989, the community office served as the village post office opening on two days only each week. In 1990, the village was granted a full-time post office.

**STOKESBY, c. 1907**

Photographed in front of the Provision Stores, owned at this time by Mrs. Eliza Smith, and showing part of The Mill Road which was a cul-de-sac. The corn-mill belonged to Mr. Edward E. Trett. It was built in c. 1826 and was operated by wind and steam power. The miller is believed to be the man in white who is standing inside the fencing on the right. The traditional Norfolk boat-shaped cap of the windmill can be identified on the picture.

**NEW ROAD, STOKESBY, c. 1914**

Until this new road was laid down in 1911 connecting the village with the main road (A1064), the villagers had to use the ferry and walk the river-wall to Acle Bridge, or take the track to the right to Billockby and Fleggburgh, crossing the Muckfleet by one of several 'liggers', which were usually single planks, en route. The New Road bridges the Muckfleet about a quarter of a mile beyond the curve, in the left background, and the track to the right eventually became disused except for cattle going to the marsh. During the 1920s and 1930s, on fine summer evenings at week-ends, villagers used to walk to Acle Bridge and back, having a drink halfway to sustain them for the return trip!

**THE APPROACHES TO GREAT YARMOUTH, c. 1900s**

An artist's impression of the river approaches to the town. Notice the corn-mill and the postmill on the right. The mill left of centre was Cobholm High Mill. It was ten-storeys high and was said to be the highest mill in the country until its demolition in 1905. The Maltings can be seen slightly to the right in the centre of the picture, with a wherry completing the scene. The population figures for Great Yarmouth and Gorleston/Southtown were 37,151 and 9,008 respectively in 1881; Great Yarmouth – 41,952, Gorleston – 12,344, Southtown – 6,422 and Runham Vauxhall – 585 in 1921; and Great Yarmouth – 49,810 in 1988.

**GREAT YARMOUTH, c. 1950**

Looking back along the River Bure, with Runham Vauxhall on the left, and showing the Yacht Station thronged with pleasure-craft. As this is the limit of navigation for these craft, the Yacht Station has been a popular overnight stop before moving on to another river within the Broadland area. In the background is Breydon railway bridge.

**GREAT YARMOUTH, c. 1936**

An aerial view of the river complex photographed before the construction of the new Great Yarmouth bypass. The exit from the River Bure can be seen centre left, and the River Yare extends out of the top of the picture, towards the mouth of the river and the North Sea. The bridge to be seen near the top is Haven Bridge; officially opened in 1931 by the Prince of Wales, who later became Edward VIII. In the foreground is Breydon Swing-Bridge, part of the rail network, with Breydon Water beyond and out of sight. Breydon Swing-Bridge opened in 1903, closed in 1953 and demolished in 1967.

**S.S. "RESOLUTE", c. 1960s**

The S.S. *Resolute* laden with holidaymakers returning from one of her two-hour cruises across Breydon Water and along the River Waveney to Burgh Castle and St. Olaves. She made three journeys each day at the height of the season, departing from Town Hall Quay, Great Yarmouth at 10.30 a.m., 2.45 p.m. and 6.30 p.m. Her last season in service was in 1979 and she was laid up the following year. Other pleasure-steamers which carried holidaymakers on day, or part-day, trips to Lowestoft, Wroxham and Norwich, included the *Oulton Belle, Yarmouth, Southtown* and *Cobholm.*

**THE BELLE STEAMSHIP COMPANY**

The Belle Steamship Co. owned a fleet of paddle-steamers and ran a service from London to the main seaside resorts along the East Coast as far north as Great Yarmouth. The fleet included the *Clacton Belle, Woolwich Belle, London Belle, Southend Belle, Walton Belle, Yarmouth Belle* and *Southwold Belle*. They were all launched between 1890 and 1900 and according to their individual size carried between 1,000 and 2,000 passengers each. Services commenced in 1870 and ran until the outbreak of the First World War; the ships operating from 1st June to September only. A timetable dated 1903 read as follows: dep. London Bridge (Fresh Wharf) – 9.15 a.m., Greenwich – 10 a.m., Tilbury – 11.15 a.m., Southend – 12.15 p.m., Clacton – 2.15 p.m., Walton-on-the-Naze – 2.45 p.m., Southwold – 5.15 p.m., Lowestoft – 6 p.m., Great Yarmouth (Town Hall Quay) – 7.15 p.m. Fares from London to Great Yarmouth in 1903 were 7/6d (38p) single and 10/6d (53p) return. Cabins were extra. The *Yarmouth Belle* is approaching her centenary and is still in service on the River Thames today.

BERNEY ARMS MILL, NORFOLK

PHOTOGRAPH BY HALLAM ASHLEY

## BERNEY ARMS MILL

Berney Arms tower mill is situated on the north bank of the River Yare, three and a half miles north-east of Reedham. It was built in c. 1865 by the Reedham Cement Company for grinding cement clinker, which was dug up at Burgh Castle and transported to the mill in wherries. The cement works closed in 1880 and the mill was converted to a drainage mill in 1883; the scoop wheel being positioned in a separate casing away from the mill. In 1951, it transferred to the Ministry of Public Buildings and Works and later, after a complete restoration lasting from 1962 to 1965, it came under the control of the Dept. of the Environment. A landmark for miles around, the 70ft-high mill, with seven floors and its machinery in full working order, is the highest marsh-mill on the Broads. Access is by boat or a half a mile walk, and open to the public from April to September. The wherry in the right foreground is the *Gleaner,* 57ft long and 14ft beam. Built in 1894 by Allen's of Coltishall and named *Orion,* she belonged for many years to Woods, Sadd and Moore of Loddon. She was sold to the Gedge family and renamed in 1922.

**REEDHAM FERRY, c. 1904**

At the time of this photograph, the ferryman was George Forder. Today the chain ferry provides the only vehicle crossing over the River Yare between Norwich and Great Yarmouth. The drainage windpump, partly obscured by the yacht overtaking the goods wherry, is now privately owned. Goods wherries, such as the one shown above, were able to transport cargoes of up to 25 tons depending on their size.

**REEDHAM, c. 1910**

Showing the swing-bridge carrying the branch line from Reedham to Lowestoft, and opened by the Great Eastern Railway Company in July 1847. (The G.E.R. amalgamated with other East Coast Group railways to become the London and North Eastern Railway Company on 1st January 1923). In the foreground is a wherry loading-stage. In the left background are the Maltings belonging to Thomas Matthew Read. Later, these were used as a bottling plant by Backs Ltd., then as a mushroom factory by The Reedham Mushroom Cultivation Co., and recently by the East Suffolk and Norfolk Rivers Authority. The Reedham Dock Co. Ltd. also had their business in the village at this time.

**RIVERSIDE AND MOORINGS, REEDHAM, 1911**

Showing part of Hall's Yard on the left of the picture. Hall's had a reputation for building fast wherries. Notice the two goods wherries: one laden and in full sail, the other brand new and probably being fitted out. The black-sailed wherry shows signs of 'better days' as there is a tear in the sail. The last Norfolk wherry to be built was the *Ella* in 1912, and by 1949 there were no trading wherries under sail. The advertising sign on the left refers to Messrs. Daniel Hurn and Sons of Norwich. They supplied a very extensive range of goods which included: yacht rope, tents and marquees, ropes, twine, sacks, stack covers, rotproof sail and awning covers, cocoa matting, netting, wagon-cart and drum covers, celebrated bell-ropes for churches, patent braided leather reins, flags of all nations, India rubber aprons, lawn tennis nets, and tents and marquees for hire. A very versatile firm!

**REEDHAM, c. 1908**

The pleasure-steamer *Water Fly* was launched in 1894. In the summer months, on weekdays, she carried holidaymakers from Yarmouth along the River Yare to Norwich, and on Sundays she provided afternoon trips from Yarmouth along the River Waveney to St. Olaves for 6d (2½p) return. She ended her service in 1914 and stripped of all her fittings, she was left decaying on the banks of Breydon Water. The postcard shows the *Water Fly* with her complement of approximately 100 passengers moored at the Ship Hotel quay. At the time, the landlord of the Ship Hotel was Mrs. Emily Anna Mutten. Mrs. Mutten was also a coal merchant, a farmer, a brick-maker and owned a wherry. She transferred the ownership of the Ship Inn to Henry Carter in 1908.

**HARDLEY, c. 1920s**

The River Yare is joined by its tributary the River Chet here at Hardley. Hardley Cross, a scheduled monument under the care of the Broads Authority, marks the boundaries of the jurisdiction of the Norwich and Great Yarmouth Corporations. A marker has stood here in some form or other since the 1400s. It was the practice of the Mayors of the respective Corporations to journey here in state barges, to make proclamations and to hear any misdemeanors committed on their respective stretches of the River Yare. The cross was repaired in 1820, 1884, and in 1899 when this fence was also erected. The cross received further attention during 1990. In the background is Norton Marshes drainage windpump built in 1863. It closed in c. 1940 and today is in the private ownership of Mr. Haylett.

**THE WATER-MILL AND THE STREET, LODDON, c. 1914**

A short detour along the River Chet leads to the small market town of Loddon. The postcard shows the old mill, the bridge over the mill-stream and The Street beyond. The water-mill was owned by Woods, Sadd and Moore in 1886. It was converted to steam power in 1888 due to its insufficient head of water. When flour milling ceased in c. 1919, many alterations were made to the mill. The loading bay on the facing side was replaced, the 'smut house', which was used to retrieve and separate rubbish coming downstream immediately behind the mill, was demolished, and the chimney was reduced to half its original height. Regarded today as 'a part of Loddon's heritage', the mill buildings house a museum, a working water-wheel, gallery, restaurant/coffee shop and antiques. The wide dyke, shown in the right foreground, was filled in during 1925–26, and now part of well-kept allotments.

**ON THE YARE, Nr. CANTLEY c. 1908**

A heavily-laden wherry running free on the River Yare. Notice the wherry has used her bonnet: an attachment of sail-cloth laced on to the bottom of the mainsail giving her a greater sail area in light winds. On the left, the drainage mill has cloth sails which are shown in the furled position. When the mill was set in operation, the miller would unfurl the cloth and spread it over the open wooden frame, tying down the ends. The windpump has long since been demolished. The population of Cantley was 266 in 1881, 291 in 1921 and 686 in 1988.

**THE SUGAR BEET FACTORY, CANTLEY, June 1912**

In 1912, the Anglo-Netherlands Sugar Corporation, the largest landowners in this area, decided to build a sugar beet factory – the first of its type in the United Kingdom – costing £170,000. The sugar beet industry had been established for some years, influenced by Dutch growers who had brought some of their workers to this country and encouraged local farmers to grow sugar beet. Cantley provided the ideal site for the new factory. It had an adjacent railway link and its close proximity to the River Yare allowed fleets of wherries to transport the crop to the factory for processing into sugar. Construction commenced on 26th March, 1912 with the building having some of the machinery from the Cos. factory at Dordrecht, Holland, which had closed in 1909. The factory chimney was topped out on 27 July, 1912 but all work was suspended when the site was inundated in the Great Flood of 28th August, 1912. The factory finally opened on 11th November, 1912 and drew its labour force of five hundred men from the surrounding countryside within a radius of fifteen to twenty miles.

**THE SUGAR BEET FACTORY, CANTLEY, June 1912**

The outbreak of the First World War caused a serious decline in production due to the lack of skilled labour and other wartime difficulties. The company was wound up in 1916 showing considerable losses, and although the factory remained closed, the machinery was maintained pending the return of favourable conditions. Production resumed during the 1920–21 season, and by 1924, the factory, a reregistered company with the same name, was processing 1,500 tonnes per day. The British Sugar Corporation was formed in 1936 with the factory at Cantley incorporated into the organisation. Sugar beet deliveries to the factory by river and rail ceased in c. 1950 and c. 1960 respectively, and today deliveries are made by road transport only. Processing traditionally commences in October, lasting for four months and producing an average of 1,000 tonnes each day. The factory employs approximately 500 workers during the season with 118 retained for maintenance work out of season.

**BUCKENHAM, c. 1912**

Buckenham is a small village north of the River Yare. At the turn of the century, the population was only 77. The postcard shows the Ferry House Inn and Buckenham Ferry which enabled travellers to cross the Yare to Claxton and Carleton St. Peter. Posted on 29th August, 1912, the sender on a yachting holiday gives details about the dreadful weather and how they were flooded out everywhere. This message refers to the Great Flood disaster in Norfolk: 7·36 inches of rain were recorded between 4 a.m. on 26th August and 9 a.m. on 27th August in Norwich. An interesting feature in the village is the very unusual 13th-century octagonal church tower. William Haslam, a former rector (1863–71) attracted vast congregations and was so popular, a special semi-circular pulpit was constructed in the rectory wall to enable him to be heard by all. The pulpit is still visible today. (Although disused, the church is in the care of the Redundant Churches Fund).

**BRUNDALL GARDENS**

Brundall Gardens were created by Dr. Michael Beverley in 1882–87. The 18-acre gardens contained many rare trees and shrubs, and its lake had the reputation of stocking the largest pike in Norfolk. Roman relics were discovered during the preparation of the Gardens and put on display in a private museum. Historians have suggested a Roman pottery kiln was sited close to the river and that Roman, Viking and Saxon ships visited and tied up at Brondale (Browndale) Hard. The Gardens became very popular between the World Wars; visitors travelling by rail to Brundall Halt, by road, and by river with pleasure-steamers tying up at the landing-stage. The Gardens were bought by Mr. & Mrs. Stringer prior to the Second World War, and were later requisitioned by the War Office and used as an Italian prisoner-of-war camp. After the war, Mr. & Mrs. Stringer took up residence again. Redclyffe House in the gardens burnt down on 2nd January, 1969 and the Gardens were bought by developers later that year. The land was resold in 1976 and forty-two houses have been built on the site.

**BRUNDALL, c. 1915**

The River Yare is reasonably deep and quite wide at this point. The postcard shows a number of craft moored in the river and a steam-powered vessel under way. Cargoes of timber, grain, or even coal for the power station, were transported to the city at this time. Today, craft of up to 500 tons (52 metres in length and up to 3·3 metres draught) still make their way up the Yare to Norwich. Craft are licensed by the Broads Authority, with a beam restriction of 3·81 metres and a scale of toll charges based on the type of usage and the block area of the vessel: i.e. the length multiplied by the beam and measured in square metres. The rivers have a speed restriction of 3, 5 or 7 m.p.h., signposted on river-banks at appropriate places.

**COLDHAM HALL, c. 1912**

At this time the proprietor of the Coldham Hall Hotel was Albert Charles Godwin. The hotel has been renowned over the years for its accommodation for visitors, riverside fishing, shooting, bathing and boating. Today, it is known as the Coldham Hall Tavern owned by The Norwich Brewery Co., and the licensee is M.R. Roberts. The house and the view on the postcard have changed very little except for the provision of ample car parking.

**SURLINGHAM**

The village of Surlingham lies to the south of the River Yare. The upper part of the village surrounds St. Mary's Church and the ruined St. Saviour's Church. The lower part of the village lies close to a wide bend in the river with a ferry crossing to Postwick, shown on the right of the picture. The Ferry House Hotel stands in the right background. It sold Youngs, Crawshay and Youngs beers and its proprietor was Henry Rawston until c. 1920. The wherry *Meteor*, shown in the foreground, is unloading coal. Along with the *Herald*, they were both owned by Samuel Barnes and carried the distinctive identification of two white bands at their mastheads. Notice the *Meteor's* hatch covers neatly stacked at each end of the hold; each cover numbered, usually in Roman numerals.

**BRAMERTON, c. 1903**

The population of the village recorded as 249 in 1881, 233 in 1921 and 310 in 1988. Bramerton lies about two miles south-west of Surlingham. The riverside scene, with people chatting, fishing or strolling along the riverbank, remains unchanged on weekend afternoons nearly a century later. The three wherries shown have been constructed to different designs. The wherry close hauled and heading downstream towards Yarmouth has a high stern sheet design: the skipper stands and steers level with the deck and the tiller curves to his waist. The two moored wherries have the more common design where the helmsman stands at a lower level holding a straight tiller. The popular Woods End Tavern nearby, known as either The Wood Inn or Wood End Hotel, is now owned by the Chef and Brewer Group. The riverside path has been converted to a narrow road and a pleasant grassed picnic area exists further along the riverbank.

**POSTWICK REACH, c. 1935**

The village of Postwick lies in a pretty vale four miles east of Norwich. A fully-laden wherry, with only a very light wind behind, is being assisted on its journey towards Yarmouth with a member of the crew using a quant; a punting pole with a disk on its end to prevent it sinking into mud. Notice the smoke rising from the cuddy; the crew's quarters in the stern, where a stove was kept lit throughout the journey to provide hot water for making tea. On the left, a mother and child pass the time at the top of the river bank.

**THORPE ST. ANDREW, c. 1950**

At the turn of the century, Mr. William A. Dutt referred to Thorpe as 'the Richmond of Norfolk'. The village is about two miles from the city centre and just outside the city boundary. The postcard shows The Thorpe Gardens Hotel which changed its name to The Boat and Bottle during the 1960s. The public house became The Rushcutter's Inn managed by Berni inns on 16th September, 1985. (For further details about Thorpe village see Norwich Vol. 2: A Second Portrait in Old Picture Postcards by Philip Standley, page 101).

**RIVERSIDE, NORWICH, c. 1912**

Downstream from Foundry Bridge, pleasure-steamers wait to depart from Riverside. A wherry, its mast lowered, can be seen moored between the two steamers, possibly waiting for its cargo of coal to be delivered by the horse-drawn coal cart belonging to R. Coller & Sons. Ranson's timber yard and the Great Eastern Hotel occupy the left bank. The same site is now occupied by the Nelson Hotel. The right bank is now occupied by Southern River Steamers, the Vagabond floating restaurant, and the *Lord Nelson* owned by the Sea Cadet Corps and the Girls Nautical Training Corps. (See also Norwich Vol. 1: A Portrait in Old Picture Postcards, page 61).

**RIVERSIDE ROAD, NORWICH**

Photographed from Foundry Bridge looking upstream along the River Wensum. A small crowd watches as the *Doris* sets off on one of her river trips. There is no other river traffic to be seen except for a few boats moored in the distance, near Bishop's Bridge. Pull's Ferry is on the left bank, obscured by the trees; the ferryman can be seen punting across the river. Today, during the peak season, it is not uncommon to see hired motor-cruisers, two abreast, moored on the right-hand bank. The city centre is only a short distance from here.

**BISHOP'S BRIDGE, NORWICH, c. 1904**

Bishop's Bridge is the oldest bridge in Norwich and was built in c. 1340 by Richard Spynk who constructed the city walls. Further navigation along the River Wensum is blocked at New Mills, a few miles upstream, near the junctions of Barn and St. Crispins Roads in the north-west area of the city. A number of goods wherries can be seen moored by the yard belonging to James Hobrough & Son, who also owned the Bishop Bridge Inn nearby. Hobrough's were contractors for dredging, pile-driving and lighterage, with the dredging of mill dams, ornamental waters and weed cutting a speciality. In the right background are Ramsey Brothers, fellmongers, hide merchants, leather dressers and wool merchants. All these buildings have now been demolished. On the extreme right, in the background, is part of a gasometer belonging to the British Gaslight Co. Ltd., now known as British Gas (Eastern Division), on Gas Hill. (See also Norwich Vol. 1: A Portrait in Old Picture Postcards, page 65).

**S.S "PRIDE OF THE YARE", c. 1907**

The *Pride of the Yare,* sister-ship to the *Queen of the Broads* (see page 4), about to pass under St. Olaves Bridge, during one of her many trips up the River Waveney from Gt. Yarmouth. During the winter months, the *Pride of the Yare* was moored here for repainting and repairs. During the Second World War both pleasure-steamers were laid up afloat at Brundall. After the war, they resumed service on the Broads but the *Pride of the Yare* was sold in c. 1947 to new owners on the River Trent. After twelve years service she was withdrawn and scrapped in 1961. The building shown in the background is The Bell Hotel whose proprietor at the time was Henry Burdock. Today, the public house is owned by Whitbreads Brewery, and the licensee is Roy Cavanagh.

**THE BRIDGE, ST. OLAVES, c. 1908**

Three bridges are known to have crossed the River Waveney at this point. The first bridge built in 1512, the second bridge built in 1768, and the steel arch bridge built in 1847 and strengthened in 1960. On the right, behind the trees, is the Bridge Stores. The thatched roof was destroyed by fire many years ago and replaced with tiles.

**ST. OLAVES, 1913**

Mr. Walter Johnson's boatyard situated close to the approach to St. Olaves Bridge. The business remained under the control of the Johnson family until it was sold in 1988 by Mr. Barry Johnson, grandson of the founder, to Mr. Roy Dethridge. The business remains a boatyard today. The picture shows the Great Yarmouth lifeboat *The John Burch* being converted into a houseboat. After its conversion it was renamed the *Crescent.*

**SOMERLEYTON**

Showing the River Waveney with the railway bridge in the background. A terrible tragedy occurred on the river here on Whit Monday morning, 1st June, 1914. Seven sea scouts of the 1st Carlton St. Mark's troop left their campsite in a sailing boat. After they had passed under the railway bridge and raised the sails, they gybed and capsized. Six were drowned and only one survived after managing to swim ashore to raise the alarm. A regatta to be held the same day was immediately postponed. The funerals were held on 5th June (five of the sea scouts were buried at Oulton Broad) and attended by an 'immense concourse'. The tragedy deeply affected the local community which remained in mourning for many months afterwards. At the inquest, the coroner recorded a verdict of accidental drowning.

**THE STAITHE, BURGH ST. PETER, c. 1914**

A rural scene which has changed completely. On the left there is now a caravan park and the inlet has a small quayheading. The Waveney Inn and its timber outbuildings are still recognisable, but the inn has now been extended to the left for use as a family room. On the right, the site is occupied by the Waveney River Centre and the Nordic Leisure Centre, providing all the necessary recreational facilities for holidaymakers to the Broads. To complete the scene, peacocks and pea-hens wander freely.

**THE OLD BRIDGE, BECCLES, p.u. 1913**

The old stone bridge was demolished in 1884. It was replaced by a steel lattice-bridge (see facing page); the single span providing easier access for river craft. The steel railway bridge, which was demolished during the 1960s, can be seen in the distance.

**BECCLES, c. 1912**

The 40-ton wherry *Emerald* being unloaded at the malthouse belonging to John Crisp and Sons. The wherry was ordered in c. 1880 by Crisp's to replace the *Garnet* which was too wide to pass under the old Beccles Bridge. Both wherries were built by Wrights of Beccles. Today, the malthouse has been demolished, the area to the left is now occupied by a car park and the inlet leads to the Loaves and Fishes Restaurant. In the background, the 97ft-high bell tower of St. Michael's Church was built in the 14th century and has a peal of ten bells.

**OULTON BROAD, c. 1912**

During the Edwardian era, yacht racing became very popular with the well-to-do. Using professional crews, sleek yachts raced each other round the Broads chasing big prize money. Oulton Broad was one of several venues where yacht racing and regattas were staged. At the time these racing machines were considered to be the fastest yachts in England with a sail area of over 1,000 sq. ft. (93 sq.m.). After the end of the First World War and during the 1920s and 1930s, these racing yachts gradually disappeared due to the high building and maintenance costs – never returning to their Edwardian heyday. By the 1930s, small boat ownership had grown rapidly and racing became a pastime for amateur sailors from all walks of life. After the Second World War, speedboat and hydroplane racing became very popular on Oulton Broad. Race meetings attracted a regular following on Thursday evenings during the 1950s and 60s. Today racing of all kinds continues on Oulton Broad. Visitors to St Olaves have the opportunity to see the only surviving classic Edwardian Broads racing yacht, the *Madie,* originally named the *Nathalie* and built in 1904, which has been extensively restored and still races on the Broads today.

**THE WHERRY HOTEL, OULTON BROAD, c. 1912**

In the left background, the buildings include malthouses and a boat-hire business. The Wherry Hotel stands overlooking Oulton Broad and before World War 1, the proprietor was Thomas Horne. Today, the hotel has been extended at the front and on the left-hand side so that the restaurant can seat over four hundred guests. Extensive plans are scheduled for this end of Oulton Broad when a proposed new road is completed. This will result in the Wherry Hotel being linked to the Nicholas Everitt Park on the opposite side of the Broad by a pedestrian bridge, where the present A146 bridges the Broad today. The Park contains a swimming pool, bowling greens and childrens playground and Oulton Broad has many moorings, boatyards and hire facilities.

**BRIDGE ROAD, OULTON BROAD, c. 1920s**

Looking down Bridge Road and showing the offices of Richard Gooch and Sam Moxey's boat-hire business, S.P. & G. Moxey – tobacconists, and the Lady of the Lake Hotel (proprietor – Edward M. Boggis). Today the original buildings have been rebuilt to house the Broadview Shopping Precinct, The Tandoori Restaurant and the Broadview Take-Away. The Lady of the Lake Tavern now has an extension to the left and is owned by the Chef and Brewer Group. The Nicholas Everitt Park and Oulton Broad are to the right, out of view, and opposite these buildings.

**THE FISHING INDUSTRY, LOWESTOFT, c. 1920s**

A reminder of yesteryear when 'the herring' was very much an industry along the east coast of England and Scotland. Lowestoft and Great Yarmouth quays would throng with drifters, locals and Scots fisherfolk from early autumn until Christmas. The postcard shows the premises of Richard Ayers Ltd., fish merchants and curers, in Whapload Road. They also had premises at 11a, New Fish Market. The lorry in the foreground, reg. no. BJ 7096, is being loaded with barrels of salted herring, with the lorry behind, reg. no. RT 2411, loaded with boxes of herring, probably kippers.

**THE YACHT BASIN, LOWESTOFT, c. 1910**

Plenty of activity to be seen with many yachts raising or furling their sails. The large building in the left background is the Royal Hotel which faces the Esplanade. On the right, overlooking the Yacht Basin, is the Royal Yacht Club.

**THE SWING-BRIDGE AND LONDON ROAD, LOWESTOFT, c. 1920s**

Journey's end to this nostalgic tour around the Norfolk Broads; one of the most beautiful areas of this country. Beyond the swing-bridge, on the right, is Lowestoft Ness – the most easterly point in Great Britain – and the North Sea.

**BROADLAND PASTIMES, c. 1910**

Published by Raphael Tuck – Scenes of Yesteryear: Series 2553 and 2696 'Shooting Incidents'.